17 44/LOB

SPORTS

RENNAY CRAATS

Weigl Publishers Inc.

Published by Weigl Publishers Inc.
350 5th Avenue, Suite 3304, PMB 6G
New York, NY 10118-0069
Website: www.weigl.com

Library of Congress Cataloging-in-Publication Data

Craats, Rennay.
 Sports : USA--past, present, future / Rennay Craats.
     p. cm.
 Includes index.
 ISBN 978-1-59036-974-6 (hard cover : alk. paper) -- ISBN 978-1-59036-975-3 (soft cover : alk. paper)
 1. Sports--United States--History--Juvenile literature. I. Title.
 GV583.C73 2009
 796.0973--dc22
                            2008023863

Printed in the United States of America
1 2 3 4 5 6 7 8 9 0 12 11 10 09 08

All of the Internet URLs given in the book were valid at the time of publication. However, due to the
dynamic nature of the Internet, some addresses may have changed, or sites may have ceased to exist
since publication. While the author and publisher regret any inconvenience this may cause readers, no
responsibility for any such changes can be accepted by either the author or the publisher.

Weigl acknowledges Getty Images as its primary image supplier for this title.

Every reasonable effort has been made to trace ownership and to obtain permission to reprint copyright
material. The publishers would be pleased to have any errors or omissions brought to their attention so
that they may be corrected in subsequent printings.

EDITOR: Heather C. Hudak
DESIGN: Terry Paulhus

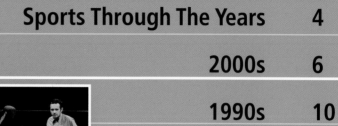

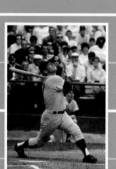

Through The Years

The United States has always had a strong sense of competition. Americans constantly make efforts to better themselves and test themselves against the best of the best.

Sports have become the perfect way to express this competitive spirit. Some sports, such as baseball, have a rich heritage and tradition, stretching back more than 100 years. Others, including the X Games, offer ways for Americans to learn new sports. Regardless of the sport, Americans have found varied and creative ways to push the limits of what the human body can accomplish.

Since the beginning of the 20th century, the United States has been home to many memorable athletes and important sporting events. Throughout this century, great contests of ability and will were played out, and champions were crowned. Through it all, the athletes of the United States pushed themselves to jump higher, run faster, and be stronger.

Whatever the future holds, U.S. athletes will continue to thrill and delight people across the country and around the world with their skill. There will be many more unforgettable moments of victory and defeat in the wide world of sports.

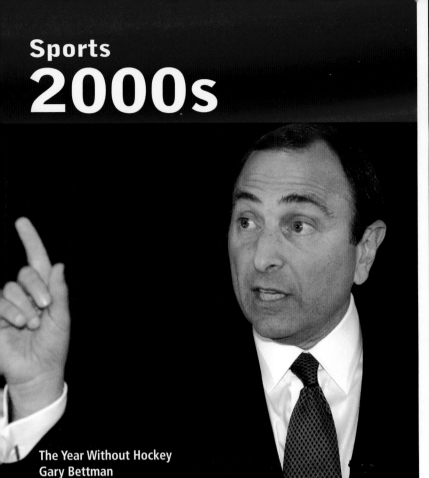

**The Year Without Hockey
Gary Bettman**

2004

Long Time Coming

One of the longest championship **droughts** in baseball history ended in 2004. Before 2004, the last time the Boston Red Sox won the World Series was 1918. Many referred to this as the "Curse of the Bambino." Babe Ruth, who was nicknamed the Bambino, was one of the best batters in the league. In 1920, the Red Sox traded Ruth to the New York Yankees. The trade was said to have cursed the Red Sox. Finally, 86 years after their last World Series victory, the Red Sox shut out the St. Louis Cardinals, winning the first four games in the series. In Boston, thousands of people took to the streets in celebration, cheering, banging pots and pans, setting off fireworks, and climbing streetlights.

2004

The Year Without Hockey

The year 2004 will be remembered by many sports fans as the year without hockey. On September 16, 2004, at the beginning of the National Hockey League's 88th season, the players went on strike, refusing to play. At the time, players were paid according to contracts they signed with their team. Contracts would promise a set amount of money, no matter how much money that player's team earned. As a result, many teams lost money if they

2001

NASCAR driver Dale Earnhart suffers a fatal crash on the track.

2002

The Los Angeles Sparks win the WNBA Championship.

could not sell enough game tickets to cover the cost of player contracts. NHL Commissioner Gary Bettman felt player incomes should be tied to team incomes in order to help teams that were struggling financially. The NHL Players' Association rejected Bettman's recommendation, and a strike was called that kept players off the ice for the entire 2004–2005 season. Eventually, an agreement was reached, and the lockout ended on July 22, 2005, too late to play any of that season's games. This was only the second time in history that hockey's championship trophy, the Stanley Cup, was not presented to a team. When the NHL returned in 2005, its rules had been changed slightly to make the game faster and more exciting for fans to watch. It was hoped that this would allow the league to gain popularity, earn more money, and keep both players and team owners happy.

2003
Sammy Sosa is the first Hispanic Major League player to hit more than 500 career home runs.

2004
Serena Williams wins the Nasdaq-100 Open.

2005
The New England Patriots win the Super Bowl.

Fighters Find Their Footing

2005

Fighters Find Their Footing

In the early 1990s, a new sport was finding its feet. With very few rules, ultimate fighting is a no-holds-barred fighting contest between men. Contestants practice mixed martial arts, using techniques from combat sports around the world, such as boxing, judo, karate, kung fu and muay thai. The first Ultimate Fighting Championship was held in 1993, but the league folded soon after. Ultimate fighting critics said that the sport was too violent and brutal to attract advertising. For the next 12 years, ultimate fighting was restricted to small venues with little television coverage. However, as time passed, additional rules were put in place, and the sport became less brutal. More fans began attending matches, and in 2005 the league, now called UFC, received dedicated television coverage for the first time. Spike TV aired a series called "The Ultimate Fighter," following the training and matches of young hopefuls over the course of a tournament. Soon, UFC events were broadcast on television and pay-per-view. In 2006, a mixed martial arts event broke pay-per-view income records, beating out both boxing and wrestling. The UFC seemed to have found its place in the spotlight.

2006

America's pastime steps outside U.S. borders as Japan defeats Cuba and wins the first World Baseball Classic.

2007

The Anaheim Ducks defeat the Ottawa Senators to win the Stanley Cup.

2006

Kobe Makes History

LA Lakers fans at the Staples Center in Los Angeles got to see history being made on January 22, 2006. In a game against the Toronto Raptors, Lakers shooting guard Kobe Bryant scored 81 points singlehandedly. This was the highest scoring total in a single game since Wilt Chamberlain's 100-point game in 1962. The Raptors had a strong first half that left the Lakers trailing by 14 points. Teammates said Kobe was very focused as the Lakers prepared for the second half. When the teams took to the court again, Kobe alone outscored the entire Toronto Raptors team. Coach Phil Jackson decided to let Kobe rest with 4.2 seconds left in the fourth quarter. The crowd gave Kobe a standing ovation as he left the court. The final score was 122–104 for Los Angeles. Kobe Bryant became one of only five players in NBA history to score more than 70 points in a single game.

Into the Future

The 2000s saw individual sports, such as running and martial arts, become more popular. These sports provide more freedom for athletes, but less support than team sports. Many athletes take part in both. Think about the sports you play at school or in your free time. Do you prefer to play on a team or as an individual? What are the benefits and disadvantages of both types of sports?

2008

Danica Patrick becomes the first woman to win an Indy Car race at the Indy 300 Japan.

2009

2010

America's Dream Team

Johnson Retires

1991

Johnson Retires

Throughout the 1980s, "Magic" Johnson had controlled the basketball court and was one of the best point guards and playmakers the game had ever known. In November 1991, he

shocked the sporting world with his announcement that he was HIV-positive. Johnson retired, became a spokesperson for AIDS awareness, and created a foundation to promote research into the disease. In 1992, he published the book, *What You Can Do to Avoid AIDS*. That year, Johnson returned to basketball at the NBA All-Star Game. After this appearance, the Lakers retired his jersey—number 32. Johnson helped the Dream Team win the gold medal at the 1992 Olympic Games in Barcelona, Spain, all the while serving on the President's Council on AIDS. Magic returned to professional basketball in September 1992, signing a contract with the Los Angeles Lakers. His return was short-lived. He became a television commentator and then the head coach of the Lakers for the 1993–94 season. Magic Johnson made one last return to basketball in 1996 as a Laker, but he retired for good after the team was beaten in the first round of the playoffs.

1992

America's Dream Team

In 1992, for the first time in Olympic history, professional basketball players were allowed to compete at the Games. Team

USA, dubbed the "Dream Team," boasted such superstars as Michael Jordan, Larry Bird, John Stockton, Magic Johnson, Charles Barkley, and Patrick Ewing. This fast-paced, exciting game was the fastest-growing sport in the U.S., and fans tuned in from home to watch their heroes playing together on the same team. The squad won all seven match-ups by an average of 44 points and spent hours signing autographs for fans in Barcelona, Spain. They easily took home the gold medal and repeated this accomplishment at the 1996 Olympics in Atlanta, Georgia.

1993

Farewell to Air

In 1993, Michael Jordan shocked fans with his announcement that he would retire from basketball. At 30 years of age, the Chicago Bulls guard was the greatest player ever. He had claimed seven straight NBA scoring titles, three straight league Most Valuable Player awards, and two Olympic gold medals. He had led the team to six championship titles and averaged a record 41 points per game in the finals in 1993. However, this year had been difficult for the king of the

1991

Rick Swenson wins the Iditarod dogsled race for the fifth time, more than any other competitor.

1992

For the first time, a non-U.S. team, the Toronto Blue Jays, wins the World Series Championship.

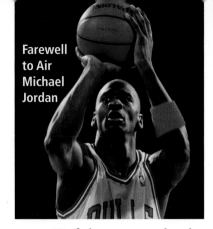

Farewell to Air Michael Jordan

Contact Sport
Nancy Kerrigan

court. His father was murdered in August, and the media swarmed with **allegations** of a gambling problem. Jordan decided to bow out of professional basketball and try his luck in baseball. A year and a half later, Jordan returned to the Bulls. Basketball fans welcomed him back with open arms. In 1996, Jordan received 2 million votes for the All-Star game, the most of any player ever. In all, he played in twelve All-Star Games and was the MVP of the game three times. Jordan again retired from the sport in 1998 as the Bulls' all-time leading scorer with 29,277 career points. He bought part of the Washington Wizards basketball team in 2000.

1994

Contact Sport

In January 1994, athletes across the country were preparing for the Winter Olympic Games in Lillehammer, Norway. U.S. skater Tonya Harding tried to ensure her medal by eliminating her rival, Nancy Kerrigan. Harding's bodyguard hit Kerrigan on the knee with a metal bar

after a practice for the Olympic trials. Harding hoped that the injury would leave Kerrigan unable to compete. Kerrigan's injuries were not serious, and she recovered. It did not take long for Harding's part in the attack to surface. While she did not face criminal charges for her actions, she was kicked off the Olympic team. She successfully sued in order to remain a part of the U.S. figure-skating team. Harding skated terribly in Lillehammer, while Kerrigan won a silver medal.

1994

A Star is Born

Venus Williams made her professional tennis debut in 1994 at 14 years of age. At the Bank of the West Classic in Oakland, California, the young player nearly knocked the number-two player out of the tournament. Her performance caught the attention of many people in the tennis world.

Her 108-mph serve shocked fans in 1996—it was the ninth-fastest serve on the tour. Williams worked hard every day to claw her way from a 211th- to a 64th-place ranking in 1997, but she had not yet won a championship. She continued to reach the semifinals in 1998 in such tournaments as the U.S. Open and the Australian Open. Then, she won her first singles title—the IGA Tennis Classic. From there, she skyrocketed to the top. Her ranking shot to number twelve in the world, and she beat established players, including Anna Kournikova, in an all-teen final. She then won the Grand Slam and set a women's world record for her 127-mph serve at the Swisscom Challenge. She and her sister, Serena, went on to make history together. In 2000, they were the first sisters ranked in the Top Ten at the same time since 1991, and they were the first sisters to win a Grand Slam crown together in the twentieth century. Williams won a gold medal in singles competition at the 2000 Olympics, as well as a doubles gold medal with Serena. She also won the Wimbledon tournament.

A Star is Born
Venus Williams

1993
Mario Lemieux is named the NHL's Most Valuable Player.

1994
The Dallas Cowboys win Super Bowl XXVIII.

1995
Cal Ripken, Jr. beats Lou Gehrig's record of 2,131 consecutive games played.

11

Fans Shut Out

1994

Fans Shut Out

In 1994, baseball fans were informed that there would not be a World Series. The players were on strike, and there seemed no hope to end it. All but two team owners agreed to cancel the season. The strike carried on for 234 days. On April 2, 1995, the two sides finally reached an agreement. The 1995 season kicked off, but not all was forgiven. Fans were angry at the strike and were slow to support their home teams.

1994

Yankees on Top

Between 1965 and 1994, the New York Yankees won only two

Yankees on Top

World Series championships. In the mid-1990s, a new wave of talented players hit Yankee Stadium like a shot. The team was back with a vengeance. Derek Jeter, Bernie Williams, and Paul O'Neill wowed baseball fans with their unstoppable hitting and unbreakable defense. The powerful pitching of Andy Pettitte and David Cone gave the Yankees the advantage they needed. In 1996, the Yankees took home the World Series championship for the 23 time in history. After losing out on a repeat the following year, the Yankees reclaimed the trophy in 1998 with a sweep of the San Diego Padres and again in 1999 with a sweep of the Atlanta Braves. David Wells achieved a perfect game in 1998, and David Cone did so the following year— no opposing player reached first base. In 2000, the Yankees became the first team in more than 25 years to "three-peat" a World Series championship when they beat the New York Mets for the title.

1997

Fierce Competitor

In 1997, Tiger Woods earned his green jacket when he won the U.S. Masters golf tournament. At 21 years of age, he was the youngest person to win the tournament. While he was at it, he broke the all-time scoring record and won by the largest number of strokes. He finished 18 under par, with a

Fierce Competitor
Tiger Woods

total of 270 points and was 12 strokes ahead of his nearest opponent. He was also the youngest player to win the Grand Slam of professional golf championships—only five players have ever achieved this feat. Among Woods' other victories were the 2000 British Open, the 2000 U.S. Open, and the 1999 and 2000 Professional Golfers Association Championships. In 1999, Woods won 11 worldwide championships. By then, he had twice been featured on the cover of Sports Illustrated as Sportsman of the Year. He was named the Male Athlete of the Year by the Associated Press in 1997 and 1999, and was ESPY Male Athlete of the Year in 1997. In 1999, Woods was named World Sportsman of the Year by the World Sports Academy. On top of this, He was Player of the Year three times. The ambitious golfer continued to win tournaments, endorse products, and set records into the 21st century.

1996

The Chicago Bulls play a record-setting regular season, winning 72 games.

1997

Baseball begins inter-league play after 126 years.

1998

The Detroit Red Wings win the Stanley Cup.

Road to Success
Lance Armstrong

1999

Road to Success

Lance Armstrong proved what it meant to be a champion. In 1991, the 20-year-old was the U.S. National Amateur Champion in road cycling, and he finished fourteenth at the Olympic Games in 1992. After that, he worked hard to compete professionally. He soon had countless titles under his belt, including the Motorola championships from 1992 to 1996, the World Championship in 1993, and the U.S. Championship in 1993. For the next few years, Armstrong rode in Europe, often the only American in the running. He won the $1 million Thrift Drug **Triple Crown** and then the 1995 Tour Du Pont, earning the title of the Velo News American Male Cyclist of the Year. In 1996, Armstrong was diagnosed with cancer, but he returned to competition in 1998 with a win at the Sprint 56K Criterium. Armstrong proved he was better than ever with victories at the Tour de Luxembourg in June and the Rheinland-Pfalz Rundfarht and the Cascade Classic in July. He finished fourth at the World Championships that year in horrible weather and racing conditions. Armstrong added an incredible chapter to his racing career in 1999, when he won the Tour de France. He repeated the winning performance six more times.

1999

Wrestlemania

In the 1990s, professional wrestling topped television ratings and attracted huge live crowds. People could not get enough of wrestlers Hulk Hogan, the Undertaker, Stone Cold Steve Austin, and Chyna. About 22 million people tuned in each week to watch. While the matches were all predetermined, the performances were athletically and physically demanding. The World Wrestling Federation, or WWF, had about 125 performers on the payroll to fight for titles and to brawl backstage. In 1999, the company earned revenues of more than $250 million. By 2000, revenues had climbed to nearly $380 million. With pay-per-view specials, home videos, and weekly shows, the popularity of professional wrestling continued to soar.

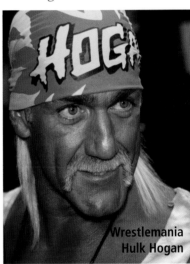

Wrestlemania
Hulk Hogan

Into the Future

Wrestling and tennis gained great popularity in the 1990s thanks to the colorful personalities of the athletes who competed in those sports. Think about athletes today. Do any stand apart from others for reasons other than their athletic skills? What makes this person special? How is he or she a role model?

1999

Tony Hawk becomes the first skateboarder to land a 900 degree rotation in competition.

2000

Tiger Woods wins the U.S. Open by 15 strokes, a record for all major golf competitions.

13

Sports
1980s

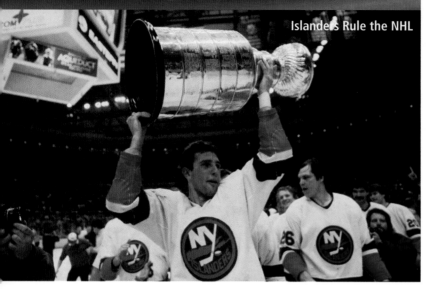

Islanders Rule the NHL

Athletes Stay Home

The 1980 Olympic Games in Moscow, USSR, were not a success. The USSR had invaded Afghanistan, and many countries were angry. U.S. President Jimmy Carter wanted to show the world what he felt about the invasion. He asked the Olympic committee to move the games out of Moscow. The committee refused. Carter decided to **boycott** the games. Fifty-nine other countries followed his lead. The boycott disappointed many athletes. They had trained hard for the competition but now could not compete at the games. They had to wait another four years for the next Olympics. It also meant that the Olympic medalists that year were not necessarily the best in the world. In response to the U.S. team's actions, the Soviet team boycotted the 1984 Olympics held in Los Angeles, California.

1980

Islanders Rule the NHL

The New York Islanders dominated professional hockey in the early eighties. Rather than trading their superstars, as many other teams had done, the Islanders recruited in small towns and from junior hockey teams. They found three important rookies in Mike Bossy, Denis Potvin, and Bryan Trottier. These men and other young, fast players led the Islanders to the Stanley Cup championships. Each line of the Islanders was strong and able to score goals. They could also defend their net, even while short-handed. In the 1983 series, the Islanders stood their ground against twenty power plays by the Edmonton Oilers. The Oilers did not score once during those power plays. On the other hand, when the Islanders had a man advantage, they put the puck in the net. In the 1981 series, the team scored a record thirty-one goals during power plays. This drive and talent helped the Islanders win the Stanley Cup for four straight seasons, starting in 1980.

Athletes Stay Home

1981	1982	1983
LeRoy Irvin returns 207 punted yards, setting an NFL record.	Pete Rose steps to home plate to bat for the 13,941st time, a Major League record.	Greg Lemond wins the World Cycling Championship.

Boys of Summer on Strike

Boys of Summer on Strike

On June 11, 1981, the baseball season came to a sudden end. Problems between owners and players resulted in a players' strike. The owners had tried to restrict free agency. Free agency allows players to have agents help them with their contracts. If they want to move, their agent helps negotiate a new contract with a new team. The owners said that free agency was costing them too much money, but the players refused to take the field without their right to become free agents. It took until July 31 to settle the strike. It was one of the longest strikes in baseball's history.

1984

Gold and Glory for Lewis

Alabama native Carl Lewis won nine Olympic gold medals between 1984 and 1996. He won four straight gold medals in the long jump. Lewis was the second Olympian in history to

Gold and Glory for Lewis

win the same event in four consecutive Olympic Games. Lewis had his best showing ever at the 1984 Olympic Games in Los Angeles. He won a gold medal in the 100- and 200-m dashes. He also helped the 4x100-m relay team win the gold. Then, he took home the gold medal in the long jump. This sort of triumph had not been seen since American Jesse Owens won four medals in the 1936 Games. Lewis became a hero, but he was not finished yet. At the 1987 World Championships, he won the long jump and was on the winning 4x100-m relay team. The next year, Lewis again won the long jump as well as the 100-m race after Canadian Ben Johnson tested positive for banned substances. Lewis finished second in the 200-meter race. Throughout his career, Carl Lewis won medals and made history. He retired from competition in 1997.

1985

Fighting to the Top

Michael Gerard Tyson learned to box in 1980. He had been sent to reform school after being charged with burglaries and robberies. Following an impressive amateur boxing career, Tyson turned professional in 1985. That year, he won fourteen bouts, eleven of which were first-round knockouts. On November 22, 1986, the heavyweight belt changed hands, when Tyson challenged the Canadian world champion, Trevor Berbick. In the second round, the powerful Tyson defeated Berbick with a sledgehammer punch. At 20 years old, Mike Tyson became the youngest world heavyweight champion ever. By 1989, his incredible win-loss record was 37-0, with 33 knockouts. Tyson was unstoppable, or at least almost so. His legal problems, including assault and rape convictions, jeopardized his career into the 1990s. After spending time in jail, Tyson returned to the ring in 1996 to win both the World Boxing Association and World Boxing Council titles. Tyson is known as one of the hardest punchers in the history of professional boxing.

Fighting to the Top Mike Tyson

1984
Michael Jordan and Charles Barkley are drafted to the NBA.

1985
The San Francisco 49ers defeat the Miami Dolphins to win Super Bowl XIX.

15

Flo-Jo Takes Olympics by Storm
Florence Griffith Joyner

Flo-Jo Takes Olympics by Storm

Since she was 7 years old, Florence Griffith Joyner had trained in track and field. She won a silver medal in the 200-m race at the 1984 Olympics, and then went into semi-retirement. She returned to track in 1987 to place second at the World Championship Games. The following year, Flo-Jo set world records at the Olympic Games. She was the first female athlete to win four medals at an Olympics. She won the gold in the 100-, 200-, and 4x100-m relay races. She also won a silver in the 4x400-m race. Her amazing performance, along with her glamorous and eye-catching style, made her a star. She became one of the highest paid sports figures in the world. Flo-Jo retired from track in 1989. She died suddenly on September 21, 1998, at the age of 38. Her passing shocked her fans and family.

American Conquers Tour de France

In 1984, Greg LeMond finished third at the **grueling** Tour de France cycling race. The Tour de France is a 2,400-mile race that takes between 25 and 30 days to complete. Fewer than half the cyclists who enter finish the course. LeMond was not satisfied with his result, although it was the best finish for a non-European cyclist up to that point. In 1986, he became the first American to win the race. A hunting accident in 1987 threatened his racing career, but he worked through the injury and competed again in 1989. He won by eight seconds—the smallest victory margin in the history of the race. LeMond went on to win the Tour de France again in 1990. A rare progressive muscle disorder forced the amazing cyclist to retire in 1994.

American Conquers Tour de France
Greg LeMond

Fall of a Hero

Pete Rose was one of the greatest baseball players ever. He played both infield and outfield, and his aggressive base running earned him the nickname "Charlie Hustle." He was the rookie of the year in 1963, and he held several records in his twenty-four years of play. He beat Ty Cobb's record for career hits, with 4,191. In 1973, Rose was named the National League MVP, and he played on seventeen All-Star teams at five different positions. Rose retired from playing for the Cincinnati Reds in 1986 and from managing the Reds in 1989. In 1989, Rose was suspended from baseball for life. He was suspected of betting on sports, including baseball. Rose insisted that he had never bet on baseball, but he agreed not to challenge the ban. In 1991, the baseball commissioner

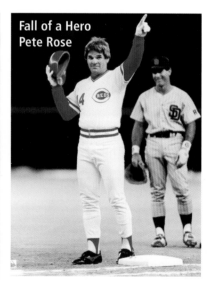

Fall of a Hero
Pete Rose

1986
Brian Boitano wins the men's World Figure Skating Championships.

1987
The U.S. men's volleyball team takes gold at the Pan American Games.

announced that anyone banned from baseball could not be inducted into the Baseball Hall of Fame. The man who had helped make baseball what it is would never be recognized. Baseball fans and Rose himself continue to petition to change the ruling. In 2004, Rose admitted to betting on the Cincinnati Reds, but never against them.

1986

Top Tennis Player

In 1982, the Women's Tennis Association ranked Martina Navratilova the world's best female player. She kept that title for four straight years. In this time, Navratilova won twelve Grand Slam tennis tournaments and boasted an incredible win-loss record of 427-14. Her strength was something not often seen in women's tennis. Her serve was clocked at 90 miles an hour. In 1975, the eighteen-year-old defected to the U.S. from Czechoslovakia. In 1986, she returned to Prague, where she led the U.S. tennis team to victory over Czechoslovakia at the Federation Cup. By 1992,

Top Tennis Player
Martina Navratilova

Kareem of the Crop

Navratilova had won over 158 championships, more than any other tennis player in history.

1989

Kareem of the Crop

Ferdinand Lewis Alcindor, Jr. led the University of California basketball team to three straight championships. This piqued the attention of the NBA, and Alcindor was offered a contract with the Milwaukee Bucks. In 1968, Alcindor became a member of the Muslim faith, and in 1971, he changed his name to Kareem Abdul-Jabbar. He played for the Bucks from 1969 to 1975.

Then, he was traded to the Los Angeles Lakers. There, the 7-feet-2-inch center led the team to five championships. Abdul-Jabbar was known for his signature "sky hook" shot. It was hard for his opponents to block, and he rarely missed. When he retired in 1989, Abdul-Jabbar was the all-time points leader in the NBA, with 38,387 in 1,560 professional games. He had led his team to the NBA finals and was named the Most Valuable Player (MVP) six times. He was one of the best players to ever take to the court and was elected to the Basketball Hall of Fame in 1995.

Into the Future

For many athletes, competing at the Olympics is a lifelong dream. Most Olympians compete for the first time between 16 and 20 years of age. Where will the Olympics be held when you are that age? Do you know anyone who is training to be an Olympic athlete?

1988

Jamie Morris makes 45 rushing attempts, the record for a single game.

1989

Jim Abbott, a one-handed pitcher, makes his Major League debut.

1990

James Buster Douglas defeats Mike Tyson.

Sports
1970s

Kings of the Ring
Muhammad Ali and Joe Frazier

1971

Kings of the Ring

Joe Frazier was an Olympic boxing champion and a fierce competitor in the ring. In 1971, Frazier was the World Boxing Association (WBA) champion. He was pitted against Muhammad Ali, the World Boxing Council (WBC) champion. Neither man had lost a bout. Frazier won the match by **decision**. Ali waited three years for a chance to fight Frazier again. In 1974, Ali beat Frazier by decision, but it was not the last time the two great boxers would meet. In 1975, Frazier and Ali faced each other in the Philippines, in a match that would become known as the "Thrilla in Manila." On October 1, around 700 million people in 65 countries watched the fight on television. Ali was incredible. Frazier's trainer threw in the towel to stop the match before the final bell. It was one of the greatest fights in boxing history. Frazier retired in 1976, leaving an impressive career with 32 victories, four defeats, and one draw. Ali went on to become one of few heavyweight boxers to win back a world championship title twice—once in 1974 and again in 1978.

1972

Swimmer's Year

U.S. swimmer Mark Spitz made history at the 1972 Olympic Games in Munich, Germany. He took the gold medal for the 100-m and 200-m freestyle. He also dominated the 100-m and 200-m butterfly races. Spitz set world records for each of these individual events. The talented athlete joined other U.S. swimmers in the 400-m and 800-m freestyle relay teams. Then, he swam the butterfly in the 400-m medley relay. His relay teams also set world records. At the end of the competition, Spitz had claimed an incredible seven gold medals for the Red, White, and Blue.

Swimmer's Year Mark Spitz

1971

Frank Shorter wins the men's marathon at the Pan American Games in Cali, Colombia

1972

At 36, Sandy Koufax becomes the youngest player to be inducted to baseball's Hall of Fame

Dolphins Undefeated

King's Court
Billie Jean King

1972

Olympic Massacre

The international camaraderie of the Olympic Games was lost at the 1972 Olympics in Munich, Germany. On September 5, eight Palestinian guerrillas, who called themselves Black September, broke into the Olympic Village. They stormed the Israeli athletes' quarters and shot and killed two coaches. In the flurry of bullets, fourteen team members managed to escape, but nine others were taken hostage. Outside, German police officers surrounded the building. The terrorists wanted the Israeli government to release 200 Palestinians imprisoned in Israel. Israeli Prime Minister Golda Meir refused to give in to the guerrillas. After negotiations, the terrorists agreed to a safe escape to Cairo with the hostages, who would then be freed. At the airport, police snipers opened fire as two of the terrorists approached the airplane. A shoot-out followed. In the end, a German police officer, five terrorists, and all the hostages lay dead. The Olympic Committee decided that the Games should continue. The rest of the Israeli team left Germany to mourn the tragedy.

1972

Dolphins Undefeated

A few professional football teams have come close to having undefeated seasons, but in 1972, the Miami Dolphins actually did it. They became the first National Football League team to finish an entire season without losing or tying a single game. With talent such as Paul Warfield, Bob Griese, Larry Csonka, and Mercury Morris, the Dolphins finished the regular season with fourteen wins, no losses. Then they won the next two division playoff games. They made it to the Super Bowl, beating the favored Washington Redskins 14-7. The Dolphins took home the title and made sporting history.

Olympic Massacre

1973

King's Court

In the early 1970s, Billie Jean King proved that she was the best female tennis player in America. She was the first woman to win more than $100,000 in competition. She paved the way for other female athletes, and she fought for equality with men's tennis. King won four U.S. Open singles titles, and she basked in a 1973 victory against Bobby Riggs. She accused him of being a male chauvinist, and she promised to teach him what a woman could do. In front of more than 30,000 stadium fans and millions more glued to their television sets, King beat the arrogant ex-champ Riggs on the court. King inspired the women's movement and fought to establish a separate tennis tour for women.

1973
HBO airs its first TV boxing broadcast.

1974
The New York Yacht Club defeats an Australian challenger four races to zero.

1975
The Pittsburgh Pirates play the highest-scoring shutout in the 20th century.

19

Hank Aaron Hits it Big

at his home diamond. Hammerin' Hank had claimed the home run record. At the time of Aaron's retirement in 1976, he held several career records, including most home runs (755), most runs batted in (2,297), and most extra-base hits (1,477). He was inducted into the Baseball Hall of Fame in 1982.

1975

Ashe on Fire

In 1975, two U.S. tennis stars competed for the Wimbledon title. The favorite, Jimmy Connors, faced off against the talented Arthur Ashe. Ashe won the match in four sets and became the first African American to win the prestigious tournament. He was also the sport's first African-American millionaire. Ashe won 51 professional tournaments, always with grace and dignity. He was forced to retire due to heart disease in 1980, and he died 13 years later.

1974

Hank Aaron Hits it Big

At the age of 15, Hank Aaron started playing shortstop for the Mobile Black Bears, a semiprofessional baseball team. The following year, in 1952, Aaron signed with the Milwaukee Braves, which would soon become the Atlanta Braves. He played his first major league game in 1954. Over the next 19 years, Aaron played well, drawing praise for both his batting and his outfielding. Meanwhile, he was nearing Babe Ruth's career home run record of 714. Late in 1973, Aaron hit his 713th career home run, but he would have to wait until the next season to try to break the record. At the beginning of the 1974 season, Aaron's first swing gave him the home run that tied Babe Ruth's record. Four days later, he hit his 715th home run

Ashe on Fire

1976
U.S. swimmer Jonty Skinner sets the first official world record in the 50-m freestyle.

1977
Bruce Wilhelm wins the first World's Strongest Man competition, held in California.

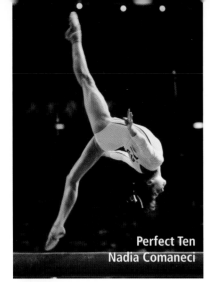

Perfect Ten
Nadia Comaneci

1976

Perfect Ten

The sweetheart of the 1976 Olympic Games in Montreal, Canada, was an 86-pound, 14-year-old Romanian gymnast. Nadia Comaneci redefined the limits of gymnastics as she flipped, twirled, and leaped her way onto the podium. She scored seven perfect 10s, the highest possible score in gymnastics. Comaneci won three gold medals, a silver, and a bronze. The young athlete went on to win several other international competitions, but none was as spectacular as her Olympic showing. Comaneci defected to the U.S. in 1989.

1979

College Hoops

On March 26, 1979, all eyes were on the National College Athletic Association (NCAA) basketball championships. The final was a showdown between Indiana State and Michigan State, but it was not the teams that drew the attention. It was the talented stars who led each side. Indiana's forward, Larry Bird, and Michigan's hero, Earvin "Magic" Johnson, were the best college players in the country. Their amazing moves and awesome talent sent college basketball television ratings through the roof. That night, Johnson came out ahead of Bird in the championship match, but their competition was not over.

The two stars carried their rivalry into the professionals, both finding great success in the National Basketball Association (NBA). Bird led the Celtics to victory three times, and Johnson dunked the Lakers to the championships five times. Each star was named Most Valuable Player in the league three times. Together, they electrified basketball fans and made it the sport to watch into the 1980s.

College Hoops

Into the Future

It was common during the 1950s, 1960s, and 1970s for athletes to become unofficial ambassadors of their countries. Athletes are trained to always conduct themselves with respect and sportsmanship. Can you think of ways these traits could be used to help unite countries or people who do not otherwise get along?

1978
Wilt Chamberlain enters the Basketball Hall of Fame.

1979
The Seattle Supersonics win the NBA championship.

1980
The U.S. men's hockey team beats the heavily favored USSR team to win Olympic gold.

Golfers Up to Par
Jack Nicklaus

1960–1969

Golfers Up to Par

Arnold Palmer became the first golfer to win the Masters championship four times. He won in 1958, 1960, 1962, and 1964. He also dominated at the Open tournaments, winning the 1960 U.S. Open and the British Open in 1961 and 1962. By 1968, Palmer had become the first golfer to claim more than $1 million in prize money. As the years passed, Palmer competed and won several Senior tournaments. He is one of the most successful and popular golfers in history. Another talented golfer, Jack Nicklaus, won his first professional tournament at the U.S. Open in 1962, beating Arnold Palmer. "The Golden Bear" won six Masters tournaments, including ones in 1963, 1965, and 1966. He was the first golfer to ever win back-to-back Masters titles. Nicklaus also walked away with five Professional Golfers' Association championships starting in 1963, as well as three more U.S. Open titles in 1967, 1972, and 1980, and three British Open titles in 1966, 1970, and 1978. He went on to win numerous Senior tournaments and made a name for himself as a golf-course architect.

1962

Scoring Machine

Wilt Chamberlain is thought to be one of the greatest basketball players in the history of the National Basketball Association (NBA). Throughout his 14-year professional career, Chamberlain claimed 23,924 rebounds and scored 31,419 points. The only player to score more was Los Angeles Lakers center Kareem Abdul-Jabbar. In 1959, the 7-foot-1-inch-tall Chamberlain was the star of the University of Kansas basketball team. He graduated and moved directly onto the squad of the NBA's Philadelphia Warriors. For his first seven seasons, he led the league in scoring. On average, he scored fifty points a game. On March 2, 1962, Chamberlain set an incredible record. He scored 100 points in a game against the New York Knicks. This record for the most points scored in a single game still stands today. The superstar was traded to the Philadelphia 76ers in 1965 and to the Los Angeles Lakers in 1968. He continued to lead his team and the league. With Chamberlain at the helm, the Lakers won the 1972 NBA title. Chamberlain was added to the Basketball Hall of Fame in 1978.

Scoring Machine
Wilt Chamberlain

1961

Roger Maris breaks Babe Ruth's home-run record, hitting 61 in a single season.

1962

The AFL championship goes to double overtime, with Dallas beating Houston by three points.

Heavy Hitting
Roger Maris

1961

Heavy Hitting

New York Yankee Roger Maris was no stranger to home plate. His team came to expect their outfielder to hit home run after home run. In 1961, Maris hit his sixty-first home run in the last game of the season. Nobody had ever hit that many home runs in a single season. To go along with this impressive record, Maris was named the American League's Most Valuable Player in 1960 and 1961. In 1966, the left-handed slugger was traded to the St. Louis Cardinals, and he retired from the game in 1968. His record remained unbroken for 37 years. In 1998, the St. Louis Cardinals' first baseman Mark McGwire, blasted 70 home runs during the regular season.

1961

Blackhawks Win the Cup

The Montreal Canadiens had won five Stanley Cup hockey championships in a row from 1956 to 1960. It seemed as though they were unstoppable. Unstoppable, that is, until Bobby Hull and the Chicago Blackhawks came along. The team had not won a championship title since 1938, and they were due for a big victory. That victory came in 1961, when Hull's blazing speed and incredible slap shot proved too much for the Canadiens. The Blackhawks managed to do what no other U.S. hockey team could do in the 1960s—they won the Stanley Cup. They have not won a championship since, but many of the team's players have set impressive league records. In 1960 and 1962, Bobby Hull was the top scorer in the league. From 1964 to 1968, a Blackhawk held the league scoring title—Bobby Hull held the record in 1966 and Stan Mikita in the other four years.

Blackhawks Win the Cup

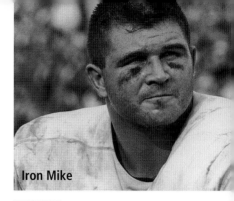
Iron Mike

1961

Iron Mike

At 122 pounds, Mike Ditka barely made his high school football team. By his senior year, he had gained 100 pounds and was a force to be feared on the field. He established himself as a linebacker, tight end, and one of the best punters in the country. Ditka also had a reputation for being intense and determined. This unstoppable quality earned him the nickname "Iron Mike." In 1961, Ditka was a first-round draft choice of the Chicago Bears. His first season was one of the best ever by a National Football League tight end—he scored 12 touchdowns on 56 catches, gaining 1,076 yards. His incredible showing earned him the rookie of the year award. In 1964, he tallied 75 catches, which was a record for tight ends at that time. In his six seasons with the Bears, Ditka made the All-Pro team four times. A few trades in the late sixties left Ditka playing for the Dallas Cowboys. He helped the team win the Super Bowl in 1971. He retired the following year with a league-record of 427 career catches.

1963
Golfer Jack Nicklaus becomes the youngest winner of The Masters.

1964
The United States wins the most medals at the Summer Olympics.

1965
Boston Celtics take the NBA finals win.

1962

Celtic Pride

The Boston Celtics **dominated** professional basketball in the 1960s. Led by stars such as Bill Russell, Tom Heinsohn, Frank Ramsey, and Bill Sharman, the team entered the sixties with a National Basketball Association championship and added another two in a row to their record. In 1962, the Celtics seemed unbeatable. The team finished the regular season with a record 60 wins. Russell was made the league MVP for the second time, becoming the first repeat award winner. In playoff competition, the Celtics met Wilt Chamberlain and the Philadelphia Warriors. In a close semifinal match-up, the Celtics managed to squeak by the Warriors and claimed another NBA championship. In 1966, they won their eighth straight NBA championship, something no other team had ever done.

Float Like a Butterfly, Sting Like a Bee

1964

Float Like a Butterfly, Sting Like a Bee

Cassius Clay was the underdog in the 1964 heavyweight championship fight. Clay had won a gold medal at the Olympics, but boxing fans thought that the bigger and meaner Sonny Liston would easily defeat him. The 22-year-old fighter knocked Liston out on February 25 with a punch so fast that many people missed it. In 1964, Clay became a Muslim and changed his name to Muhammad Ali. When the Vietnam War draft board came calling, Ali refused to join the army because of his religious beliefs. He was stripped of his championship title as a result. In 1970, the fighter won a court appeal that reversed the decision. Four years later, Ali defeated George Foreman to reclaim his title as "the greatest." He became a role model for many young men.

1965

Broadway Joe

In 1965, the University of Alabama's star quarterback Joe Namath shocked the country. He snubbed the National Football League to join the New York Jets of the new American Football League. To show how happy they were about his decision, the Jets gave their starter a contract worth $400,000. It was the highest-paying professional sports contract ever at the time. Namath proved that he was worth every penny. He promised fans that he would lead his team to the 1969 Super Bowl, and he did. He was named the Most Valuable Player and won the S. Rae Hickok award as the athlete of the year. In the off-season, Namath launched his acting career. He appeared in several films and television programs throughout his athletic career. This interest earned him his nickname, Broadway Joe. Namath retired from football in 1978, but he stayed involved in the sport through television broadcasting. His knowledge and strong personality made him a star. Namath was inducted into the Pro Football Hall of Fame in 1985.

Celtic Pride

Broadway Joe

1966

The Baltimore Orioles win the World Series.

1967

The Green Bay Packers defeat the Dallas Cowboys in an event now called the Ice Bowl.

1968

The sport of Ultimate Frisbee is invented in New Jersey.

Olympic Statement

Queen of the Ice
Peggy Flemming

1968

Olympic Statement

The racial tensions in the U.S. carried over into the 1968 Olympic Games in Mexico City. Two African-American athletes, Tommy Smith and John Carlos, competed in track and field. Smith finished first, and Carlos finished third in the 200-m race. Instead of celebrating U.S. victory, the two athletes criticized the lack of civil rights in their own country. To protest racism in their country, neither man looked at the flag as the "Star-Spangled Banner" played. Each held a black-gloved fist in the air as a sign of Black Power.

Their statement did not impress the U.S. Olympic committee. The men were suspended from the Games and were ordered to leave Olympic village immediately. The image of the defiant men on the podium became a symbol of racial discontent in the sixties.

1968

Queen of the Ice

At 15 years old, Peggy Fleming won her first U.S. Senior Ladies' figure-skating championship. She went on to win the next four titles in a row. In the North American championships, Fleming finished second in 1965 and then first in 1967.

She struggled to win the world championships in 1965—but came in third. After training hard, she won the championships for the next three years. In 1968, Fleming represented the U.S. at the Winter Olympics in Grenoble, France. She skated the performance of her life and was rewarded with the gold medal. After the Olympics, Fleming turned professional. She skated with such groups as the Ice Capades, Holiday on Ice, and Ice Follies.

Into the Future

Muhammad Ali inspired many people with his strength and intelligence. He was a strong-willed man who was proud of his heritage and had great confidence in his future. Many people find athletes to be positive role models. Can you think of any people in your life who encourage you to try harder and achieve success?

1969

Diana Krump becomes the first American woman jockey to race against men.

1970

Joe Frazier begins his heavyweight championship winning streak with a victory over Jimmy Ellis.

The Stuff of Legends

1950–1959

The Stuff of Legends

The New York Yankees won eight division pennants and six World Series championships between 1950 and 1959. They did so with the leadership of two All-Star players—Yogi Berra and Mickey Mantle. Berra was a famed Yankees catcher. He played in 15 All-Star games in a row and was the league's Most Valuable Player in 1951, 1954, and 1955. Berra held several records, including the career home-run record for catchers. He won fourteen pennants and ten World Series championships in his incredible eighteen-year career—more than any other player. He was famous for his

sayings, which he spouted off behind the plate to distract batters, entertain umpires, and inspire his teammates. His determination and never-say-die attitude was summed up by his famous adage, "It ain't over 'til it's over." He retired in 1965 but stayed a part of the game as a coach and manager. Mickey Mantle had big shoes to fill when he replaced Joe DiMaggio in centerfield in 1951. Despite injuries and a bone inflammation in his leg, Mantle led the league six times in runs scored and four times in home runs. Mantle held the batting title in 1956 and won the Triple Crown the same year. He was voted Most Valuable Player in 1956, 1957, and 1962. Through the twelve World Series championships in which he

competed, Mantle set records for most runs, most home runs, most runs batted in, and total bases batted in regular season and play-off competition. Mantle retired in 1969. Both he and Berra became baseball legends and were inducted into the Baseball Hall of Fame.

1950

Basketball Dynasty

The National Basketball Association (NBA) was formed in 1950, and the Minneapolis Lakers were part of it. That season, the team battled the Rochester Royals for the division title and breezed through the semifinals. With players such as George Mikan, Jim Pollard, Bud Grant, and Vern Mikkelsen, the Lakers seemed unstoppable. They beat the Syracuse Nationals to win the first NBA championship and their second championship in a row. Most critics pegged the Lakers as the favorites the following year, but

Basketball Dynasty

1951

Joe DiMaggio plays his final regular season game.

1952

The Detroit Lions defeat the Cleveland Browns to win the NFL championship.

1953

The first Basketball World Championship for Women takes place.

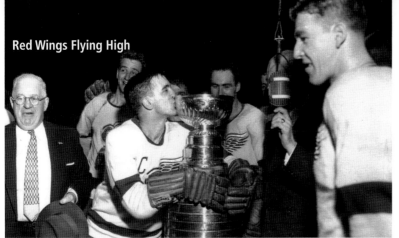

Red Wings Flying High

the Royals clinched the division title. The Lakers were not discouraged. They came back in 1952 and 1953 to beat the New York Knickerbockers for top honors. The Lakers were the first repeat champions in the league. The Lakers were a team to fear in the NBA. In 1954, they defended their championship again with a win against Syracuse. At the end of the season, the league introduced the 24-second time limit to shoot and a foul limit per player and per team. These new elements of the game, along with the loss of veteran players, hurt the Lakers. Their dynasty was over. They did not win another championship in the 1950s.

1950

Red Wings Flying High

Canadian teams had dominated hockey through the 1940s. In the 1950s, the Detroit Red Wings changed that. Despite an injured Gordie Howe, the Red Wings started out the decade with a Stanley Cup win in 1950. Howe recovered through the off-season and returned to the team,

but they could not defend their championship. In 1952, Terry Sawchuk made his goaltending debut in the finals and was a star. He shut out the Montreal Canadiens in two games and held them to only two goals in total during the four-game series. The Red Wings had won another Stanley Cup. After losing the title to Montreal in 1953, the Red Wings came back to win it again in 1954. This time, the team successfully defended its title with another Stanley Cup win in 1955. Then, the streak ended for decades. The Red Wings would not win another Stanley Cup until 1997.

1951

Queens of the Court

American tennis players made international news in the 1950s. Maureen Connolly won her first National Women's title in 1951 at the age of 16. The following year, she won at Wimbledon and went on to defend her U.S. title. Then, in 1953, she became the first woman and second person ever to win the Grand Slam—

top honors at the British, U.S., Australian, and French championships all in one year. Connolly continued to shine in 1954, winning the French and Wimbledon championships. Before the U.S. championships, she had a serious horseback-riding accident that ended her career. She passed on her tennis knowledge and skills through coaching others. Althea Gibson was another star athlete in the fifties. In 1950, she played in the tennis circuit in New York, which was previously made up only of players of European ancestry. Then, in 1957, she became the first African American to win the prestigious Wimbledon tournament. Gibson also claimed titles at the French, Italian, U.S., and Australian Opens. She was named the Female Athlete of the Year in 1957. The following year, Gibson repeated her reign as the Wimbledon and U.S. national champion. Tennis was not her only strength—she joined the Ladies Professional Golf Association in 1963.

Queens of the Court
Maureen Connolly

1954

The Minneapolis Lakers win the NBA championship over the Syracuse Nationals.

1955

The U.S. men's volleyball team wins the gold medal at the Pan American Games in Mexico City.

1951

Willie Mays

On May 25, 1951, the New York Giants turned their eyes to rookie Willie Mays to help them win games. The team expected great things from this young, talented ballplayer, and so did the fans. When Mays got up to bat for the first time, he struck out. In the next twenty-six trips to home plate, he got only one hit. Fans turned their backs on him, but Mays soon caught their attention. He suddenly began to live up to everyone's expectations. He caught, threw, and batted with dazzling talent and was named Rookie of the Year in 1951. For the next two seasons, Mays served in the U.S. Army and then came back better than ever. He continued to amaze fans as he led the Giants to a World Series victory in 1954. That year, he was honored with the title Player of the Year. He led the league in stolen bases from 1956 through 1959 and led the National League in home runs in 1955, 1962, 1964, and 1965. When he retired in 1973, Mays had been the first player to hit 300 home runs and steal 300 bases. He was also the first National League player to hit 600 home runs in his career. He is considered one of the best baseball players ever.

1952

Marciano a Knock-out

Rocco "Rocky" Marciano began boxing in the U.S. Army and then launched a professional boxing career in 1947. In 1951, the strongman cried after knocking out Joe Louis, his boyhood hero. In September 1952, Marciano became the world heavyweight champion by knocking out Jersey Joe Walcott. Marciano had been losing that fight, but he came back with a flurry of punches that showed both his strength and his incredible determination. Between 1953 and 1955, Marciano defended his title successfully six times. He retired in 1956 when he was 33 years old. During his professional career, he won forty-three professional bouts by knockout. His final tally was forty-nine wins, no losses. Marciano was the only heavyweight champion to have a perfect record.

1953

Golf Legend

Golfer Ben Hogan had been the leading money winner several

Willie Mays

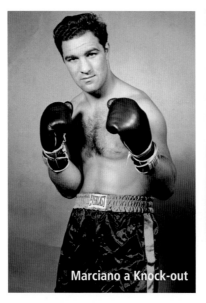

Marciano a Knock-out

Golf Legend
Ben Hogan

1956

Don Larsen pitches the only perfect game in World Series history.

1957

Americans win the men's and women's world figure skating titles.

1958

The Baltimore Colts win the NFL title.

seasons during the 1940s. He was thought to be one of the greatest golfers ever. In 1949, Hogan was nearly killed when his car was hit by a bus. Doctors thought he might not walk well again. He surprised everyone. Only seventeen months later, in 1950, Hogan won his second U.S. Open championship. He won the tournament again in 1951. Then, in 1953, he crushed the record for the tournament by five strokes. That year, he went on to win the British Open as well. Throughout his career, Hogan won more than sixty tournaments and set a standard for future golfers.

1956

Pitch Perfect

Pitcher Don Larsen had struggled to become a starting pitcher with the New York Yankees after being sent back to the minor leagues in 1955. Manager Casey Stengel believed in Larsen and knew he would come through for the team. After a few disappointing games in the

**Pitch Perfect
Don Larsen**

1956 World Series, fans demanded that Larsen sit on the bench. Stengel had other ideas. Larsen started the fifth game of the series against Brooklyn on October 8. As the innings passed, people realized that

no one had hit safely off Larsen yet. He had not walked a batter, either. Could he become the first ever to pitch a perfect game in the World Series? Many thought it impossible but held their breath anyway as Larsen kept throwing strikes. As he delivered a final strike to end the game, catcher Yogi Berra ran to the mound to celebrate. Larsen had done it! The Yankees were the champions, and Larsen had made history. He set a record by pitching the first no-hitter in World Series history. He also pitched a perfect game—not one batter had reached first base. Throughout nine whole innings of play, Larsen threw only ninety-seven pitches.

Into the Future

Basketball gained popularity in many cities because it can be played almost any place and does not require much equipment. Are there any other sports that are easy to place indoors or outside? How did these sports begin? Where are they played today?

1959

U.S. swimmer Michael Troy beats the world record for the 200-m butterfly twice in one day.

1960

Bill Mazeroski of the Pittsburgh Pirates becomes the first player to end the World Series with a home run.

**Olympic Heroes
Dick Button**

1940–1948

Olympic Heroes

The Olympic Games scheduled for 1940 and 1944 were cancelled because of the war. Many members of the International Olympic Committee felt that the 1948 Games should be cancelled as well. The things that had happened during the war went against the Olympic ideal of universal peace. Despite these concerns, London, England, still recovering from the war, hosted the Summer Games in August. The Olympics were a huge success, especially for U.S. athletes. They chalked up 662 points and 38 gold medals. Second-place Sweden trailed with only 353 points. Bob Mathias proved to be one of the biggest stars of the games. The 17-year-old decathlete endured a grueling contest to take home the gold. The 1948 Winter Olympic Games in Saint Moritz, Switzerland, also brought medals home to the U.S. At the games, Dick Button became the first American to win an Olympic gold medal in figure skating, and Gretchen Fraser became the first American to take home Olympic medals in alpine skiing. She won a gold medal in slalom and a silver in the alpine-combined competition.

1941

King of Diamonds

Joltin' Joe DiMaggio was tearing up the base paths in 1941. The New York Yankee outfielder hit safely in 56 straight games. His streak ended with a double play in the eighth inning on July 17. DiMaggio finished that season with thirty home runs and 125 runs batted in. He was a leader, often being at the top of the league in batting, home runs, and runs batted in. DiMaggio was more than a great hitter—he was also one of the best outfielders ever to play the game. His strong skills led the Yankees to nine World Series titles, including the championship in 1941, 1947, and 1949. He was named Most Valuable Player of the American League in 1939, 1941, and 1947. Joltin' Joe played for the Yankees from his rookie year in 1936 until his retirement in 1952, except for the three years he spent serving in the Army. America's fascination with this quiet hero did not end with his retirement

**King of Diamonds
Joe DiMaggio**

1941

Ted Williams becomes the last major league baseball player to bat over .400.

1942

President Roosevelt urges baseball teams to play more games at night so war factory workers can attend.

from baseball. He captured the country's imagination when he married screen goddess Marilyn Monroe in 1954. They divorced later that year. DiMaggio had a big impact on U.S. society and culture. Even after his death in 1999, he remains a baseball legend and a hero to many.

1942

Fantastic Footballer

Many people say that Don Hutson was the first true wide receiver in National Football League history. He signed with the Green Bay Packers in 1935 and enjoyed playing for one of the few teams that focused on passing the ball rather than running it down the field. His first professional play had him catching an 83-yard touchdown pass. Opposing players soon came to fear Hutson. He became the first player to be covered by several defenders at the same time. With Hutson at the helm, the Packers battled to four division titles, including one in 1944, and two NFL championships. In 1942, Hutson set the league season scoring record, with 138 points. In the Green Bay Packers star's eleven-year career, he was the league's top scorer five times and its best receiver eight times. He netted top honors as the Most Valuable Player in 1941 and 1942. When he retired in 1945, he had 488 career catches, 7,991 yards, and 99 touchdowns to his name. Hutson was made a

Fantastic Footballer
Don Hutson

member of the Football Hall of Fame when it was established in 1963.

1943

Bears Devour Competition

The Chicago Bears began the decade with a championship win over the Washington Redskins. The "T" formation created by the coaches offered the quarterback protection and allowed for an easy hand-off. This prevented the Redskins from scoring. The Bears, including Sid Luckman and Harry Clark, defended their title in 1941 against the New

York Giants. The following year, they finished the regular season without a loss but lost the play-off championship to the Redskins, 14 to 6. In 1943, the team fought back to the top. With Sid Luckman's leadership, the team reclaimed the championship in a victory over Washington. Washington's Sammy Baugh gave the game his all—in 1943, he became the first player to intercept four passes in a game. Still, he could not compete with Luckman's arm. Luckman was the first professional player to pass for more than 400 yards in a single game. After two years of not making the finals, the Bears returned to take back the championship. In 1946, Sid Luckman and Ken Kavanaugh led the team to victory over the Giants. The Bears would have to wait until 1963 before they would win another championship.

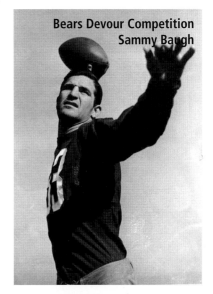

Bears Devour Competition
Sammy Baugh

1943
The Chicago Bears win the NFL championship.

1944
Joe Nuxhall, age 15, becomes the youngest player to pitch a Major League game.

1945
World War II prevents many sporting events from being held.

31

Girls of Summer

Girls of Summer

Hundreds of Major League players joined the military during the 1940s. In 1943, Chicago Cubs owner Phillip Wrigley founded the All American Girls' Professional Baseball League (AAGPBL). Teams from across the Midwest competed in major-league parks, and their popularity soared. Fans soon realized that the girls could really play, and thousands paid to watch their favorite teams. The players had special rules. Each player attended charm school, where she learned beauty tips and **etiquette**. The rules stated that she always had to be dressed in feminine clothes off the diamond—no pants or shorts. Long hair was preferred, and lipstick was a must. On the field, players had to wear baseball skirts rather than pants, a style that offered no protection for women's legs when they slid into a base or dove after a ball.

Other than these rules, the women's game was very similar to the men's. Women used a smaller ball and a shortened field. They started out pitching underhand, but, by 1948, pitchers were throwing overhand. The game was exciting and outlasted the return of U.S. soldiers and baseball players. This did not last for long, though. Televised baseball games and financial problems led to the AAGPBL's end. The league was dissolved in 1954, but it remains a unique part of baseball history.

1946

New Basketball League

In 1946, a group of New York executives created a new professional basketball league called the Basketball Association of America (BAA). This new league had teams in New York City, Boston, Philadelphia, Chicago, and Detroit. It competed with the National Basketball League (NBL), which had been established in the mid-thirties. Just as the 1948 season was about to begin, the four best

New Basketball League

teams in the NBL—Minneapolis, Rochester, Fort Wayne, and Indianapolis—joined the BAA. The following year, the six remaining teams switched to the BAA. A three-division league called the National Basketball Association (NBA) was created. In 1949, the Minneapolis Lakers was the first team to win the new NBA championship title. In 1950, the NBA cut its size so that the teams would fit into two divisions. These later became the Eastern and Western conferences that were established in 1970. The NBA remained strong throughout the rest of the century, and well into the next.

1947

Breaking Barriers

On April 15, 1947, in front of 26,500 fans, Jackie Robinson became the first African American to play in the major leagues of baseball. The road was not easy. Many of his teammates petitioned to have him removed from the field. There was talk that some teams would refuse to play the Dodgers if Robinson was in the game. As Robinson blazed around the bases, his opponents tried to **spike** him. He received death threats, and people often yelled at him. Despite these distractions, Robinson was named National League Rookie of the Year and led his team to the World Series. It did not take long for Robinson to prove himself a star. His batting was consistently great,

1946
Lloyd Magnum of Texas wins the U.S. Open.

1947
A radio announcer names the wrong horse as winner of the Preakness in Baltimore.

1948
Three MLB teams are fined $500 each for recruiting high school players.

Breaking Barriers

he played many positions well, and he was one of the most talented base runners in the game. In 1949, he was named the Most Valuable Player, and other African Americans began joining major league teams. In 1962, Robinson became the first African American inducted into the Baseball Hall of Fame.

1947

Joe Louis, Heavyweight Champion

Joe Louis, nicknamed "The Brown Bomber," won his first professional boxing match with a knockout in 1934. Three years later, he fought his way to the top as the heavyweight champion. During his career, Louis won sixty-eight fights and only lost three. Fifty-four of these victories were by knockout. One especially tough loss was to German boxer Max Schmeling in 1936. The Nazis used the win to argue Nazi superiority. In a rematch two years later, Louis made his country proud by winning the bout in one round. The country celebrated, and Louis was a hero. He became a champion of the war, giving inspiring speeches and helping the government recruit people for service. The competition for the championship title was suspended in 1942—Louis had volunteered for service. "The Brown Bomber" hung up his gloves in 1949 after eleven years as boxing's heavyweight champion. He had defended his title twenty-five times. At 35 years old, Louis did not have the powerful jab and hook that once struck fear into his opponents. After losing to Rocky Marciano in a 1951 comeback, Lewis retired from boxing for good.

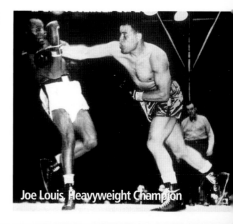
Joe Louis, Heavyweight Champion

Into the Future

Baseball is sometimes called "America's favorite pastime." It is played all over the nation and the world by all ages and skill levels. Why do you think this sport is so popular? What other sports that have a huge following around the world? Why?

1949
Bill Holland of North Carolina wins the Indy 500.

1950
Horseracing's National Museum of Racing and Hall of Fame is founded in Saratoga Springs, New York.

Sports
1930s

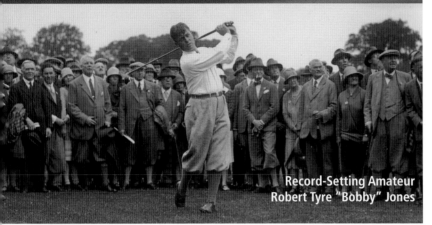

Record-Setting Amateur
Robert Tyre "Bobby" Jones

The Iron Horse Says Goodbye

Lou Gehrig was the Pride of the Yankees, and 60,000 fans showed up at Yankee Stadium to prove it. Through the years, Gehrig had led the league in runs batted in, and he broke the league record in 1931 with 184. He had also made an amazing 23 grand slam home runs, which was a major league record. On July 4, 1939, Lou Gehrig bid a final farewell to the game he loved and the fans who loved to watch him play it. He was too sick to play. Before this, Gehrig had never missed one of the 2,130 games that made up his fifteen seasons as Yankee first baseman. He had fought his way through injuries and illness, continuing to give his all to his team. His determination had earned him the nickname the Iron Horse. His illness was diagnosed as amyotrophic lateral sclerosis (ALS), which is a disease that affects the nerves. It causes muscles to deteriorate and results in **paralysis** and death. Before his death from ALS in 1941, Gehrig was inducted into the Baseball Hall of Fame. The disease became commonly known as Lou Gehrig's disease.

1930

Record-Setting Amateur

Robert Tyre "Bobby" Jones was an Atlanta lawyer who enjoyed playing golf. He won the U.S. Open championship four times and was the U.S. national amateur champion five times. The golfing lawyer also took home the British Open title three times. In 1926, Jones became the first person ever to win both the U.S. and British Opens in the same year. Then, in 1930, he made history. He became the first person ever to win the Grand Slam by winning the Open and Amateur titles in Britain and the U.S. The U.S. Amateur championship turned out to be his last tournament. After taking home the prize and entering the record books, Jones retired from the sport without ever becoming a professional. Four years after his retirement, Jones founded the Masters tournament, which has been played by golf legends ever since.

The Iron Horse Says Goodbye
Lou Gehrig

1931

Baseball's Negro National League disbands.
The St. Louis Stars win the last championship.

1932

The United States wins the most medals
at both the Summer and Winter Olympics.

Fan Favorite
Jay Dean

1932–1935

Fan Favorite

Jay Dean, better known as Dizzy, was famous for his incredible pitching. He led his league in strikeouts from 1932 to 1935 as the St. Louis Cardinals' prized pitcher. His brother Paul, known by the equally wacky nickname of Daffy, joined the Cardinals' pitching staff in 1933. Dizzy won thirty games for his team and, with the help of his brother, led the team to a World Series victory. The team was known as the Gas House Gang for its aggressive style of play. In 1938, Dizzy left the Cardinals and began playing for the Chicago Cubs. An injury to his arm that same year took away his fastball, but that did not mean batters easily hit off him. He became baseball's best slow-ball pitcher. His change-up would have batters winding themselves into the ground and staring at the ball in the catcher's mitt. Dean finished the season with seven wins and only one loss, leading the team to the World Series playoffs. The charismatic ball player retired in 1941, but he did not stray far from the game he loved. He worked as a radio and television commentator, bringing the games to fans at home. In 1954, Dizzy Dean's achievements were honored with his induction into the Baseball Hall of Fame.

1932

Blackhawks Take Wing

The Chicago Blackhawks hockey team was founded in 1926. It did not take the new team long to show what it was made of. The Hawks did so with the help of the best and most exciting goaltender, Charlie Gardiner. In 1932, he won the Vezina Trophy for having the fewest goals-against average. He was also an All-Star. The following year, the goaltending was not the only unstoppable part of the team— the rest of the squad was solid, too. Doc Romnes, Paul Thompson, Much Marsh, and Clarence "Taffy" Abel led the team to victory. Gardiner again won the Vezina Trophy, boasting ten games in which the other team did not score. The Blackhawks were the league champions in 1934, walking away with the Stanley Cup. Over the next few years, the team rebuilt after Gardiner's death from a brain tumor at the age of 29. The Hawks replaced him with Mike Karakas and added Earl Siebert, the best defenseman in the league. The team fought through the playoffs and defeated the Montreal Canadiens and the New York Americans to face the Toronto Maple Leafs in the finals. The Chicago Blackhawks repeated their earlier victory by winning the 1938 Stanley Cup. The team would have to wait until 1961 before they claimed the coveted prize again.

Blackhawks Take Wing

1933

The first ski-racing trail in North America is created on Cannon Mountain, New Hampshire.

1934

The New York Yacht Club defends the America's Cup from its British challenger.

1935

Detroit teams win the NFL, NHL, and MLB championships in one year.

Conquering the Court
Helen Hull Jacobs

championships in 1932, 1934, and 1935. Jacobs competed at the Wimbledon tournament six times, claiming the championship in 1936. For 12 years, she was ranked in the top 10 in the world. Helen Hull Jacobs was more than a terrific athlete. She was also practical. In 1933, she broke with tradition and became the first female tennis player to wear shorts during competition. In response to the reaction to this **controversial** move, Jacobs replied simply, "It seemed like the sensible thing to do."

Golden Age for Baseball

1933

Conquering the Court

Helen Hull Jacobs captured her first national junior tennis championship in 1924. She battled against her rival, Helen Wills, throughout her career. Wills beat her in the 1928 finals at Lake Forest and then again in the Wimbledon match-up the following year. Even though Wills often came out on top during these competitions, Jacobs's was a fan favorite. She had charisma and personality. Jacobs's only victory against Wills came in 1933. Wills was behind and then withdrew from the match due to a back injury. After Wills's retirement, Jacobs was able to shine without the shadow cast by her rival. She won four singles titles in a row from 1932 to 1935. She also boasted a mixed doubles victory in 1934 and three doubles

1935

Golden Age for Baseball

The 1930s saw many firsts connected with baseball. Lights were added to stadiums, and the first night game was held. Fans could now cheer on their favorite players after work. In 1935, the Chicago Cubs' owner became the first to have all the team's games broadcast over the radio. Faraway fans, as well as those who could not make the games, could now enjoy the sport almost as if they were there. The thirties also marked the opening of the Baseball Hall of Fame. Its first members were named in 1936. Babe Ruth, Ty Cobb, Honus Wagner, Christy Mathewson, and Walter Johnson were the first stars to be honored as Hall of Famers. It took another three years before the hall itself was completed. It came in perfect time. It was the 100th

anniversary of the game in 1939. The Baseball Hall of Fame opened its doors in Cooperstown, New York, on June 12. Cooperstown was believed to be where the game had been invented by Abner Doubleday. Ever since, memorabilia—including jerseys, souvenirs of important games or achievements, equipment, and photographs—have tracked the development of the game and its players. The Hall of Fame houses more than 6,000 baseball artifacts and has a library containing an enormous collection of literature and material about baseball.

1936

Track and Field Triumph

Adolf Hitler was positive that German athletes would dominate the 1936 Olympic Games in Berlin because they were superior people. Jesse Owens proved him wrong. The African-American athlete took home four gold medals. He won gold medals in the 100- and 200-meter races, the 400-meter relay, and the running broad jump. The U.S. relay team broke the world's record with a time of

1936
Jockey Ralph Neves is mistakenly pronounced dead in a horseracing accident.

1937
Wally Parks forms a club considered to be the start of organized drag racing.

Track and Field Triumph

39.8 seconds with the help of Owens. He also held the running broad jump record from a competition in 1935. His Olympic jump was less than 3 inches shy of that record. While Owens was named Athlete of the Games, the host country's leader refused to recognize his achievements. Hitler would not award Owens his medals because of the athlete's color. Hitler was also disappointed with the U.S. for using "auxiliary helpers" to win medals. He said that without these African Americans, Germany would have rightfully claimed its medals. Despite Hitler's ideas, Owens was an instant American hero and entered the record books as one of the greatest athletes ever.

1937

Grand-Slamming Raqueteer

Don Budge was an all-round great tennis player. He had a textbook-perfect backhand and powerful strokes that kept him winning matches in the 1930s. In 1937, Budge took home both the U.S. Open and the Wimbledon singles championships. At Wimbledon, he won all the titles—he was the singles, doubles, and mixed doubles champion. He then successfully defended his titles the following year. Budge also twice helped the U.S. win the Davis Cup, an international men's team competition. In 1938, Budge entered the history books. He became the first tennis player to get a grand slam. He won the Wimbledon tournament as well as the French and Australian singles championships all in the same year. After this incredible accomplishment, Budge turned professional.

Grand-Slamming Raqueteer

Into the Future

The sport of hockey began in Canada, but it was not long before the game made its way south. The United States and Canada have competed in the NHL for many years, creating a strong and friendly rivalry. What sports do you play with or against your friends? How does this affect your relationship?

1938
Johnny Vander Meer becomes the only pitcher ever to throw two no-hitter games.

1939
The National Baseball Hall of Fame is dedicated.

1940
The racehorse Seabiscuit wins its final race.

1920

The Great Bambino

George Ruth, better known as Babe, remains one of the most popular athletes in history. He was known throughout the world for more than his talent on the baseball field. His charisma attracted many fans. Japan even declared a "Babu Rusu Day" to honor the New York Yankee outfielder. He had many nicknames, including "Bambino," which is Italian for "babe," and the "Sultan of Swat" for his powerful bat. In 1920, the Yankees offered Ruth the amazing sum of $125,000 to play for the team. The following year, he smashed fifty-nine home runs over the fence. This made him even more popular in New York. The new stadium was

officially named Yankee Stadium, but it was commonly called "The House that Ruth Built." Ruth won ten home run titles and helped the Yankees win four World Series championships. During the playoffs in 1926, Ruth heard about a young fan in hospital. He wrote the boy a telegram, promising to hit a home run for him that day. He did better than that. He hit three. Ruth held many Major League records. In 1927, he hit sixty regular-season home runs—a record that would last until Roger Maris hit sixty-one in 1961. Ruth's career home run record of 714 stood until 1974, when Hank Aaron broke it. In his twenty-two years as a professional baseball player, Babe Ruth played 2,503 games, had a batting average of 0.342, drove in 2,213 runs, and was walked 2,056 times. He is often thought of as the best player to ever walk on the diamond.

1920

Tilden All Aces

"Big Bill" Tilden lobbed and aced his way into the record books in 1920. He was the best and most powerful tennis player of the time. In 1920, Tilden won the U.S. National Singles Championship. He defended

Tilden All Aces

that title five years running. For the entire decade, Tilden was part of the U.S. Davis Cup team. He contributed to seven championships in a row, from 1920 to 1926. In 1920, he became the first U.S. player to win Britain's Wimbledon tennis championship. He won it again in 1921 and 1930. By 1929, Tilden had reclaimed the U.S. singles championship and also taken the singles titles in Switzerland and the Netherlands. Tilden won many doubles titles as well, including those in 1921, 1922, and 1927. He took the mixed doubles championships four times, including the 1922 and 1923 contests. By the time Tilden turned professional in 1931, he had a record sixteen U.S. championships under his belt. Bill Tilden completely dominated tennis throughout the twenties and made it more than a country-club event. It was always an exciting spectacle when "Big Bill" was on the court.

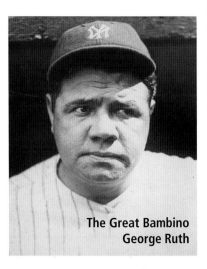

The Great Bambino
George Ruth

1921
"Behave Yourself" wins the Kentucky Derby.

1922
The American Professional Football Association becomes the NFL.

1923
Jack Dempsey defends his heavyweight title with a knockout against Luis Firpo in round two.

Caddy Shows His Stuff

years, the magazine had sponsored a bodybuilding competition, and Atlas had won both times. The contest was stopped because the magazine figured that Atlas would win every time. He had built his perfect body using what he called "dynamic tension," or isometrics. This is a technique that tenses one muscle group in opposition to another group or against immovable objects. By 1927, Atlas's enormous build was enormously profitable. He offered help to others who wanted to bulk up. His mail-order business earned the bodybuilder $1,000 each day.

1922

Caddy Shows His Stuff

Gene Sarazen started playing golf as a young boy. As well, he used to **caddy** for other golfers so he could earn money and still be around the game. In 1922, when he was twenty-one, he won the U.S. Open and the U.S. Professional Golfers Association (USPGA) championships. He was the first golfer to win both titles in the same year. He defended his USPGA title in 1923. From 1927 to 1937, he was also a member of the Ryder Cup teams. Sarazen competed in exhibitions for the rest of the decade, but he did not win another major tournament until 1932. Then he won the U.S. Open and the British Open. In 1935, he won the Masters tournament. This made him the first golfer to have won the four major tournaments of the time— the British Open, the Masters, the U.S. Open, and the USPGA.

At the Masters, he made one of the best-known shots in the history of the game—he got an albatross, which is three strokes under par, on the fifteenth hole, tying him for the lead. Famed as one of the greatest golfers of the 1920s and 1930s, Sarazen was elected to the Professional Golf Association Hall of Fame in 1941.

1922

Building Better Bodies

Charles Atlas was born Angelo Siciliano. As a child, he was small and timid. The 97-pound weakling was tired of being bullied, so he trained as hard as he could to build muscle. He used the statues of Hercules he saw in the Brooklyn Museum as his inspiration. After years of hard work and training, Atlas was successful. In 1922, Physical Culture magazine named the 28-year-old the "World's Most Perfectly Developed Man." For two

Building Better Bodies
Charles Atlas

1924
The United States wins 99 medals at the Summer Olympics in Paris, France.

1925
The Pittsburgh Pirates earn a World Series win against the Washington Senators.

39

Iron Wills

1922

Iron Wills

Helen Wills was one of the best female tennis players in the history of the game. During her long career, she won nineteen singles titles at tournaments around the world. In 1922, at the age of sixteen, Wills surprised the tennis community by making it to the U.S. championship finals. She played without emotion, earning her the nickname "Little Miss Poker Face." Her powerful forehand made her virtually unbeatable during the 1920s. In 1924, Wills won gold medals in singles and doubles competitions at the Olympic Games in Paris, France. She took home the U.S. women's singles championship seven times. In Britain, she dominated the Wimbledon championships, taking home the top prize in 1927, 1928, 1929, 1930, 1932, 1935, and 1938. Her success continued in France, where she won the singles titles in 1928, 1929, 1930, and 1932. Wills retired in 1938. She was inducted into the U.S. Lawn Tennis Hall of Fame in 1959.

1924

America Joins the NHL

In 1924, the Boston Bruins became the first U.S. team to join the National Hockey League. Other American teams soon followed. In their first game, the Bruins beat the Montreal Maroons 2–1, but this victory was not a sign of things to come. The Bruins lost the next eleven games. Despite the goal-scoring power of Jimmy Herberts, the team finished the season in last place. The following season, the Bruins improved their record, but not by much. They ended up fourth. Their third year in the league, the Bruins battled their way to the Stanley Cup playoffs, but lost to the Ottawa Senators. Big names, including Eddie Shore, Harry Oliver, and Frank Frederickson, drew fans to the arena and put points to the scoreboard. In the 1927–28 season, the Bruins won the Prince of Wales Trophy for their first-place finish in the American Division, but they were knocked out of the playoffs by the New York Rangers. In the 1928–29 season, all the Bruins' hard work

America Joins the NHL

was realized. The first championship final between U.S. teams resulted in a Bruins victory. They won their first Stanley Cup on March 29, 1929.

1924

The Galloping Ghost

For nearly twenty years, Harold "Red" Grange ruled the football field. He enrolled at the University of Illinois to play baseball and basketball. His fraternity brothers convinced him to go out for football instead. Number seventy-seven made the coaches notice him—to introduce himself, he returned a punt and scored a 65-yard touchdown. From then on, Grange was a local celebrity. Previously, college football had been a campus interest. Now it was a city-wide sensation followed by millions of people. In his first year, Grange was named an All-American. He was given that honor twice more before graduating. In 1924, the talented halfback scored five touchdowns the first five times he received the ball. This prompted sportswriter Grantland Rice to dub him the "Galloping Ghost." With Grange's help, the University of Illinois dethroned the college kings of the gridiron. Its victories over the University of Michigan in 1924 and the University of Philadelphia in 1925 went down in the history books. During his time at the university, Grange scored thirty-one touchdowns in twenty games. After graduating, he

The Galloping Ghost

signed football's first big professional contract with the Chicago Bears. He was offered $100,000 and a share of the admission profits. Most other footballers were making $25 to $100 per game. Grange retired from the sport in 1934 and was inducted into the Pro Football Hall of Fame in 1963.

1927

The Long Count

On September 22, 1927, about 150,000 excited boxing fans filled Chicago's Soldier Field. This was a record showing for a sporting event. The draw—the heavyweight championship match between champ Gene Tunney and challenger Jack Dempsey. Tunney had taken the title from Dempsey the year before, and it was advertised as the grudge match—Dempsey wanted his heavyweight belt back. It did not take long for Dempsey to take control. He sent Tunney to the canvas with blow after blow, but he did not return to his corner after knocking Tunney down, as the rules stated he must. The referee would not start the count until Dempsey was in his corner. It took Tunney until the count of nine to get to his feet again. A count of ten would have been ruled a knockout, ending the match in Dempsey's favor. Tunney came back to win the match. Fans and sports journalists claimed that Tunney had an unfair chance to recover from the attack because the count did not start until five seconds after Tunney had been knocked down. The match became one of boxing's most controversial and was dubbed the "Battle of the Long Count." After this loss, Dempsey retired from boxing. Tunney retired in 1928 with an undefeated heavyweight record.

The Long Count

Into the Future

In the early part of the 20th century, athletes used much less protective equipment than they do today. As technology and medical knowledge improved, athletes became better protected. The trend to find new, safer equipment continues today. Think about the sports you play. How has the gear you used changed since you first played the sport? In what ways can it continue to improve?

1928
The New York Rangers win the Stanley Cup.

1929
Roy Riegels runs the wrong direction in a Rose Bowl game, leading to the other team's victory.

1930
The first World Cup of Soccer is held.

1910–1915

Athletics Rule the Diamond

The Philadelphia Athletics won the World Series championships in 1910, 1911, and 1913. They also battled for the title in 1914 and 1915. Frank "Home Run" Baker was one reason for the success. He was one of the year's top five home run hitters in the American League seven times. He was also at the top for runs batted in. During his rookie year in 1909, he earned a .305 batting average and led the league in triples. Baker's two home runs and .375 series average led the Athletics to the championship in 1911. In 1913, he hit 12 home runs, 117 runs batted in, and had an average of .450 during the World Series match up. Baker played for the Athletics until 1916. He was traded to New

York and finished his career as a Yankee. Pitcher Charles "Chief" Bender was another key Athletic during the 1910s. Rather than work his way through the minor leagues, he shot directly to the top of the majors. On May 12, 1910, he delivered a no-hitter to the Cleveland Indians, thanks to a new pitch he had developed. It was a hard curveball that became known as a slider. His strong arm helped the team win the championship. He was the first pitcher to win six championship titles. Bender retired in 1917, finishing his career with an earned run average of 2.46 and with 212 wins and 127.

1913

Forward Pass

Before the success of its football team, the small South Bend, Indiana, college of Notre Dame

Forward Pass

was virtually unknown across the country. Then, star players Knute Rockne and Gus Dorais arrived and put the school on the sports map. Notre Dame's team was small, and the coaches were looking for a way to make up for that. Rockne, the team captain, suggested they try the forward pass. The forward pass had been used since 1906, but it was not often brought into college play. As a result, few other teams would know how to defend against this strategy. In a game against fearsome Army, Notre Dame's forward passing proved itself a huge success. Notre Dame beat the larger and stronger team 35 to 13. This upset launched the school to the

Athletics Rule the Diamond

1911

The Chicago Cubs defeat the New York Giants to win the World Series.

1914

The first international figure skating championship is held in New Haven, Connecticut.

top of the football ranks and changed football forever. More teams began using the forward pass, making it a basic part of the game.

1911

Speedy Racer

Ray Harroun lived for speed. He earned his living with it, too. In 1911, he entered the history books at the first Indianapolis 500. At the time, the automobile race was called the International 500 Mile Sweepstakes. On May 30, 1911, Harroun started his engine in 28th position on the track. Six hours, forty-two minutes, and eight seconds later, Harroun crossed the finish line, having traveled at an average speed of 74.602 miles per hour. He was the first winner of the prestigious race. He took home $10,000 of the total $25,000 prize money for the race. Since 1911, the Indianapolis 500 has been run every year except during World War I in 1917 and 1918 and again during World War II from 1942 to 1945. Today, the race draws more than 350,000 spectators, who watch 33 drivers circle 500 miles around the track.

Speedy Racer

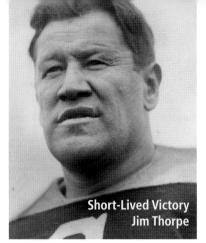
Short-Lived Victory
Jim Thorpe

1912

Short-Lived Victory

Jim Thorpe was one of the greatest athletes in the 1910s. This Native American from Prague, Oklahoma, could do it all—football, baseball, lacrosse, archery, hockey, boxing, and tennis. In track and field, Thorpe was unbeatable. At the 1912 Olympic Games, Thorpe set a world record score of 8,412.955 points. He won another gold medal in the pentathlon event. Six months after the Olympics, it was discovered that Thorpe had earned $25 a week playing minor-league baseball during the summers of 1909 and 1910. This made him a professional athlete and not eligible to compete at the Olympics. Thorpe's appeal to the Amateur Athletics Union was refused. His gold medals were taken from him, and his records were erased. The athletes who had finished second supported Thorpe. They refused to accept the gold medals. Still, Thorpe was voted the best athlete of the first half of the century in 1950.

He went on to play professional baseball in Boston and New York and football in Canton, Ohio. In 1982, the International Olympic Committee restored Thorpe's records and presented the gold medals to his children the following year.

1913

Golf For the Public

Before 1913, golf was a game reserved for wealthy people. That changed when Boston's Francis Ouimet stepped onto the green. The 20-year-old golf caddy entered the U.S. Open tournament. He defeated prominent British golfers Harry Vardon and Ted Ray in 18 holes to win the tournament. This is thought to be one of the largest sport upsets of the 20th century. Besides earning Ouimet a reputation as a talented golfer, the victory brought international attention to both the tournament and the sport. In 1916, the Professional Golfers' Association of America (PGA) was established, and annual tournaments began immediately.

Golf For the Public

1917

The Seattle Metropolitans win their first Stanley Cup.

1918

Babe Ruth leads the American League in home runs.

1919

The Green Bay Packers football team is formed in Wisconsin.

Denton True Young

1908

Hard-Hitting Heavyweights

Jack Johnson was not intimidated by Tommy Burns, the world heavyweight boxing champion. For two years, Johnson challenged Burns to a bout. In 1908, the title match between Johnson and Burns finally arrived. Johnson fought hard. His strength and raw ability overpowered Burns, the smallest heavyweight champion ever. The police stepped in to stop the intense beating. Johnson claimed the title after a battle that had lasted 14 rounds. With the decision, Johnson became the first African American to win the heavyweight crown. Johnson went on to defend his title until 1915, when he lost to American Jess Willard in round 26.

1900s

Denton True Young

Denton True Young had a fearsome fastball. It earned him the nickname Cyclone—Cy for short. Young was the best pitcher baseball ever knew. He began his career in Cleveland when he was 23 years old. In his first game, Young allowed only three batters to hit and led his team to an 8–1 victory. Young left Cleveland for the St. Louis Cardinals in 1898 and then joined the Boston Red Sox in 1901. In 1903, Boston was fighting for the World Series title. In game five, the team put its hopes on Young. He allowed only six batters to hit, and he hit three of his own for good measure. The Sox won the game 11–2. In his three starts during that series, Young won two of them and helped his team to victory in the first World Series championship. On May 5, 1906, Young became the first pitcher in the Major Leagues to pitch a perfect game— no opposition player reached first base. He boasted no-hitters three times in his 22-year career. Young averaged 27 wins per year and had an earned-run average of only 2.12. Young holds the league record for complete games (751), career wins (511), and innings pitched (7,356). He retired in 1911 and was inducted into the Baseball Hall of Fame in 1937. Each year, the Cy Young Award is given to the best big-league pitcher.

1900

Outstanding Olympians

The 1900 Olympic Games were held in Paris, France. More than

Hard-Hitting Heavyweights

Outstanding Olympians

1901
Minor baseball associations around the country form Minor League Baseball.

1902
Luis Castro, the first Latin-American to play professional baseball, debuts with the Philadelphia Athletics.

1,200 athletes arrived from 26 countries to compete for the silver and bronze medals—there was no gold medal during the decade. University of Pennsylvania roommates Alvin Kraenzlein, Irving Baxter, and John Tewksbury were joined by Lafayette, Indiana, native Ray Ewry to form an incredible track-and-field team. They controlled the 23 track-and-field events, winning 11, finishing second in five, and third in one. Kraenzlein is the only track athlete to win four individual titles in one year. Baxter led the medals with two first-place finishes and three second-place finishes. U.S. athletes also took home medals in other events. The polo team shared a victory with Great Britain, and the tug-of-war team claimed second place. In golf, Charles Sands won the men's singles event. The coxed eights rowing team also won their event. The 1900 games were the first to allow women to compete. American Marion Jones finished third in women's singles tennis, and Margaret Abbott won the women's singles golf title, with Daria Pratt placing third.

1906

Football Fatalities

Before 1906, football teams relied on brute strength and outweighing the opposition to win games. In 1904 alone, there were 18 deaths and 159 injuries during college football games. Several colleges banned or

threatened to ban football. Then, in 1906, the Intercollegiate Athletic Association made a number of rule changes to try to make the game safer. One of these changes was to allow the forward pass. The association also created a new neutral zone. This area lay between the offensive and defensive lines. Also, the offense now had to have at least six players on the line of scrimmage before the play was started.

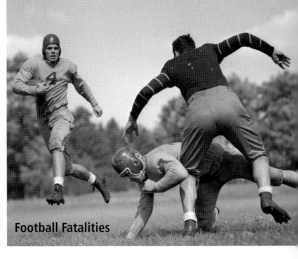

Football Fatalities

1906

Marathon Fiasco

The marathon lost some of its luster at the 1904 Olympic Games in St. Louis, Missouri. One runner was chased a mile off course by a dog, and the hot weather prevented 17 of the other 31 racers from finishing. In the end, American Fred Lorz was the first to cross the finish line, but officials soon discovered that Lorz had not finished at all. At the 9-mile point, he had suffered from cramps and dropped out of the race. An official drove him to

the stadium to get his street clothes. Lorz decided to run in and break the winner's tape as a joke. He carried the gag too far by accepting the winning medal. Lorz was banned from competition but was reinstated the next year. The true winner of the marathon was American Thomas Hicks. He finished the race in three hours, 28 minutes, 53 seconds. That is the worst marathon time in Olympic history. Hicks was helped over the finish line. In a final twist to the marathon, Cuban Felix Carvajal, competing in his street clothes, paused at an apple orchard for a snack. He became sick from the rotten fruit and had to rest. He eventually got up and stumbled to the finish line. He still came in fourth.

Marathon Fiasco

1908
Major League Baseball has its lowest-scoring season.

1909
Monte and Abe Attell become the first brothers to hold world boxing titles at the same time.

1910
John McDermott wins golf's U.S. Open.

45

ACTIVITY
Into the future

Since humans have been on Earth, they have played sports and games. Sports are invented by creative people who are looking for ways humans could interact with their environment in fun and challenging ways. There are many different types of sports, but most have some basis features in common.

An important part of any sport is a set of rules for play. Some sports, such as running or skateboarding, only need rules when athletes come together to compete with one another. Most team sports, however, must be played within a specific set of rules. Baseball, soccer, and basketball are examples of team sports that have firm rules in place. Rules may include penalties for people who behave poorly during the game or standards by which points are scored.

Another important part of any sport is its equipment. Some sports require very little gear. For example, track athletes need only have a good pair of running shoes. To play full-contact sports, such as football or hockey, athletes must wear full sets of pads and protectors. Balls of all shapes and sizes are common, as are specialized play items such as pucks and badminton shuttles.

Invent a Sport

Think about the sports you play on a team or as an individual. What are your favorite parts of each sport? What equipment do you need to play? Are there special rules for the game? Now, try putting these pieces together to form a new sport. Many great sports have been created by making small changes to existing sports. Your sport could involve a change to the rules of a game you know already. What if you could use your hands in a soccer match or replace a football with a frisbee or hula hoop? Making these changes to sports you know well can create an entirely different pastime. You also could try inventing a new sport. To do this, imagine how your sport will be played and the equipment you will need. Is it a team sport or do people play as individuals? How many people or teams take part in each game? Will you need special equipment, such as protective gear or a ball? Once you have made a set of rules, try testing your invention by playing with your friends.

FURTHER
Research

Many books and websites provide information on sports. To learn more about this topic, borrow books from the library, or surf the Internet.

Books

Most libraries have computers that connect to a database for researching information. If you input a key word, you will be provided with a list of books in the library that contain information on that topic. Non-fiction books are arranged numerically, using their call number. Fiction books are organized alphabetically by the author's last name.

Websites

To learn more about sports in the United States, visit **http://usa.usembassy.de/sports.htm**.

For interactive sports information, surf to **www.sikids.com**.

Glossary

allegations: claims that a person has done something wrong or illegal

boycott: to show disapproval by refusing to have dealings with an organization or government

caddy: a person who carries a golfer's clubs

controversial: disputed

decision: a judge's ruling on the winner of a boxing match

droughts: a long period without something

etiquette: the rules of behavior in society

grueling: very tiring

paralysis: unable to move any part of one's body

spike: slide into a base with cleats up in an attempt to injure the baseplayer

Triple Crown: when a baseball player leads in home runs, runs batted in, and batting average in a season

Index